THE ZENNED OUT

SOUL
DISCOVERY
JOURNAL

**YOUR PERSONAL GUIDE TO
UNDERSTANDING YOUR ENERGY,
INTUITION, AND THE MAGICKAL WORLD**

CASSIE UHL

ROCK
POINT

INTRODUCTION **4**

⟡ **6** ⟡

CHAPTER 1

ENERGY

CHAKRAS **8**
AURAS **20**
THE FOUR ELEMENTS **30**
ASTROLOGY **40**
PROTECTION RITUALS **51**

⟡ **60** ⟡

CHAPTER 2

INTUITION

TUNE INTO YOUR INTUITION **62**
ORACLE AND TAROT CARDS **70**
PALMISTRY **80**
NUMEROLOGY **90**
RUNES **100**

· ◦ ▷ **108** ◁ ◦ ·

CHAPTER 3

MAGICK AND SPELLWORK

HERBS AND PLANTS **110**
CANDLE MAGICK **120**
MAGICKAL DAYS **127**
MOON PHASES **136**
CRYSTALS **147**

ABOUT THE AUTHOR **159**

···◇ INTRODUCTION ◇···

Discovering your unique spiritual path is something to be celebrated because it feels like coming home. If you're reading this, I have a hunch that you've gotten a taste of that and you now feel compelled to continue exploring the terrain of your soul on a deeper level.

Understanding yourself on a soul level can help shine a light on your unique spiritual path. Like mine and those of many others I know, your path probably won't be quick or easy, but it will be yours, and it will be meaningful. Those elusive moments, or spiritual awakenings, when everything seems to click and make sense are your guideposts along the way. My hope for you is that this journal will be full of little guideposts steering you as you travel your distinctive journey.

YOUR INNER CALLINGS ARE WHISPERS FROM YOUR SOUL, HOPING YOU'LL CONTINUE TO EXPLORE AND FORGE YOUR OWN PATH.

The most important thing I hope that you'll remember is that it's okay to change your mind. You are allowed to change. I started meditating and working with my energy at a young age. Fortunately, I had an open-minded grandmother who made me feel safe to explore this part of myself. I spent much of my teenage and adult years exploring all different avenues of spirituality, including yoga, Buddhism, meditation, divination, astrology, energy healing, witchcraft, and more. I learned something from every part of my journey. I also made mistakes and got it wrong sometimes, and still do!

Regardless of mistakes or detours on my spiritual journey, I've continued as a forever student, always learning and expanding. The pull to sink deeper into my personal spiritual path has gotten stronger. I believe this can be true for you too.

Allow yourself to be pulled where you want to go in this journal. You do not need to follow it in order, answer every question, or perform every exercise (but if you do, that's fine too!). You can repeat as many exercises as you like either on a separate piece of paper or in a blank journal. I encourage you to spend a few minutes looking at the table of contents. As you do, notice which topics jump out to you the most. I also encourage you to notice which topics you may have an initial aversion to, as there may be wisdom to be found there too. Go to where you're called first and see how your energy feels as you dive into that topic, and then every topic as you go along.

This world needs more people like you—people who want to listen to the whispers of their soul, even when it veers from a previous path; people who want to heal themselves so they can help heal others and the world around them.

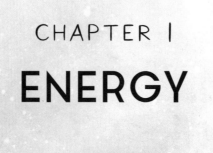

CHAPTER I

ENERGY

There are so many forces that work within us and around us that we can't see. Gravity, sound, and magnetism are all invisible but very real energies. Subtle energy is the unseen force you sense when your intuition is piqued. It is the energy of emotions, thought, and inner knowing. You have an entire subtle body system designated to these unseen energies, and even more outside of you. Your subtle body is the unseen system that's responsible for the flow of energy within and around you. It holds the pieces of you that are eternal, the parts that will live on when your physical body dies. Understanding your subtle energy body is empowering. It gives you the necessary tools to understand, clear, and protect your energy.

Every person and thing you come in contact with is energy that you engage with, and it will affect you and your unique energetic makeup differently. The four elements—earth, air, water, and fire—can each be called upon to shift the energy of yourself or your environment. The energetic makeup of your energy body, which includes the chakra system and aura, says a lot about you and how you engage with the world. The study of astrology also has an energetic effect on you. Astrology offers an energetic blueprint of the moment you come earthside and affects day-to-day energy.

Chakras, the aura, the four elements, and astrology are all tools. Tools to help you know yourself, feel more balanced, and understand your unique gifts. This section offers you an opportunity to learn about various energetic topics. Once you learn techniques to better understand and balance your energy, you'll want to protect it. This chapter ends with an ever-important section on energy protection.

···◆ CHAKRAS ◆···

The chakras are seven intangible wheels of energy aligned vertically in the center of your body. The word *chakra* is Sanskrit and translates to "wheel." Though the term *chakra* originated in early Hinduism and Buddhism, there are references to different energy centers throughout the body in cultures worldwide. For better or worse, the term *chakra* has become the most common word to describe energy centers throughout the body. However, I always encourage people to explore what the energy centers are in their own heritage.

For the vast majority of us, the subtle body is something that is felt but not seen. Each chakra corresponds with different parts of your physical body and different aspects of living. The subtle and physical bodies are intrinsically linked and affect each other moment to moment. For example, if the physical body experiences trauma, the trauma can be stored in the subtle body.

WHEN YOU UNDERSTAND YOUR ENERGY BODY,
YOU WILL GAIN A DEEPER UNDERSTANDING
OF YOUR SOUL.

There are three primary parts of the subtle body: the nadis (channels of energy), the chakras (wheels of energy), and the aura (energy that radiates outside of the body). All three systems are intimately connected to each other and the physical body. Also, note that the three primary nadis are Ida, Pingali, and Sushumna, and they interact with the chakra system the most. To understand the chakras, it's helpful to have a basic understanding of the entire subtle body system.

The chakras are in constant motion, exchanging energy between the nadis and the aura. When the chakras are out of balance, this affects the entire subtle body, which can eventually manifest in the physical body, too.

These wheels of energy are all over your body, and there are far more than just the seven primary chakras. The number of chakras in a human body varies from culture to culture and text to text. Some early texts suggest there are as many as 114 chakras within the subtle body, but within this journal, I'll be focusing on the seven primary chakras.

◁◝ THE SUBTLE ENERGY BODY ◝▷

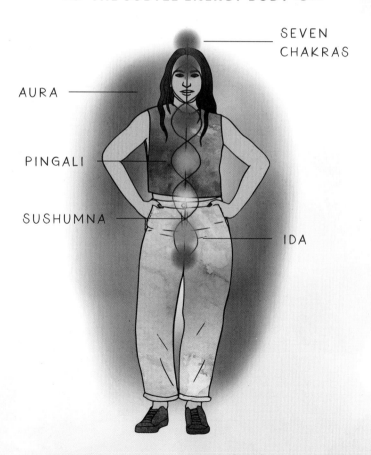

SEVEN
CHAKRAS

AURA

PINGALI

SUSHUMNA

IDA

◀⌣ THE SEVEN CHAKRAS ⌣▶

Each of the seven primary chakras relates to physical parts of the body, including prominent nerve bundles, glands, and organs. On a nonphysical level, each chakra also corresponds to light and sound. Light and sound are both vibratory frequencies. As we move up the chakra system from base to crown, the vibration increases. The sounds and colors associated with each chakra increase in vibration as well.

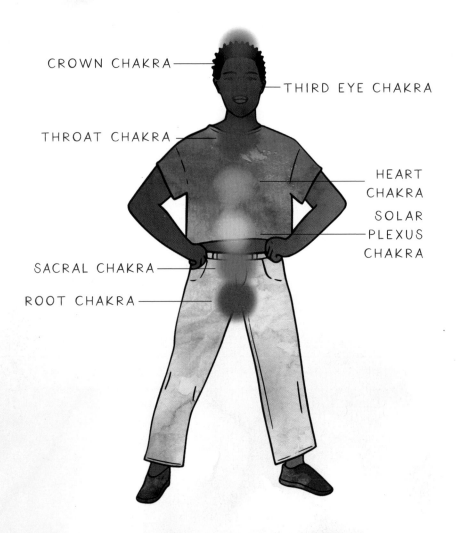

CROWN CHAKRA

THIRD EYE CHAKRA

THROAT CHAKRA

HEART
CHAKRA

SOLAR
PLEXUS
CHAKRA

SACRAL CHAKRA

ROOT CHAKRA

CROWN CHAKRA

Placement: Top of head
Colors: Rainbow, white, gold

THIRD EYE CHAKRA

Placement: In between eyebrows
Colors: Indigo, purple

THROAT CHAKRA

Placement: Throat
Colors: Blue, turquoise

HEART CHAKRA

Placement: Center of chest
Colors: Green, pink

SOLAR PLEXUS CHAKRA

Placement: Diaphragm area, above the navel
Colors: Yellow

SACRAL CHAKRA

Placement: Below the navel, pubic area
Colors: Orange

ROOT CHAKRA

Placement: Base of spine
Colors: Red, black

When your chakras are blocked, overactive, or underactive you will most likely feel this imbalance. Imbalances can manifest in many ways and will present differently for everyone depending on the nature of them. When you are more aware of your energy body, you can experience greater emotional, mental, physical, and spiritual ease. Properly cared for, your chakras help keep you emotionally, mentally, and physically well.

·•◇ TIP ◇•·

You can use crystals to help you restore an imbalanced chakra. Place crystals on your body where the coordinating chakra is, carry them in your pocket, or hold them during meditation. See page 147 to learn more about crystals.

◁◞ ROOT CHAKRA EXERCISE ◟▷

Your root chakra is your direct link to the Earth and your ability to be grounded and feel secure. To strengthen your connection to your root chakra, go outside and firmly plant your feet on the ground or sit down. If you can't go outside then imagine yourself stepping outside. Take a few slow breaths, closing your eyes if you're comfortable doing so. Begin to open your eyes and focus on one object. Record what is currently in front of you. Do this exercise whenever you need help staying grounded.

What do you:

SMELL	
HEAR	
FEEL	
SEE	

⊰⌣ SACRAL CHAKRA EXERCISE ⌣⊱

The sacral chakra is responsible for your ability to experience pleasure and work through your emotions. This chakra connects with the element of water and governs creative energy. Creative energy doesn't always mean painting or drawing and could include growing a life inside of you, collaborating with others, or creating a physical item. This area calls you to tune into what brings you joy and to relish in it.

What activities make you feel the most creative and joyful?

◄⌣ SOLAR PLEXUS CHAKRA EXERCISE ⌣►

Your solar plexus chakra is your powerhouse of energy and transformation. The purpose of the solar plexus chakra is to transform, energize, and empower you. This chakra corresponds with the element of fire. The fiery energy associated with this area offers you the power and confidence to accomplish your goals, call upon your willpower, and continually transform yourself to better align with your soul.

What can you do in your daily life to feel more empowered?

·◁〜 HEART CHAKRA EXERCISE 〜▷·

Your heart chakra is your key to fully loving and accepting yourself and those around you—flaws and all. Your heart space is the lower and upper chakras' meeting point, creating a beautiful balance of energy. This balance of energy is often referred to as a bridge. It connects the more physical energy of the lower chakras and the more ethereal energy of the upper chakras. The heart space invites us to find a balance of giving and receiving love for ourselves and others.

In what ways do you share love with others and with yourself? Are the ways that you give and receive love balanced?

◄◡ THROAT CHAKRA EXERCISE ◡►

The throat chakra gives you the tools you need to express yourself on a soul level. It is your seat of communication and expression. The throat chakra relates to the element of air. Like air, your voice may not be visible, but it is still powerful. Bringing your throat space into balance will enable you to communicate more authentically, express yourself more powerfully, and listen more deeply.

Write three things that you'd like to express but haven't had the confidence to yet.

1.

2.

3.

◁◠ THIRD EYE CHAKRA EXERCISE ◡▷

Your third eye chakra enables you to understand the world, rather than wondering and questioning—it is the seat of intuition and psychic abilities. It enables you to focus more intently in all areas of both your inner and your outer worlds. Everyone is intuitive and has psychic abilities to some degree, and like all of the energy centers of the subtle body, the wisdom of the third eye can also be cultivated.

Write about the last time you experienced an intuition or gut feelings/messages. Did you feel it in a specific part of your body, did you have an inner knowing, or did you hear or see something in your mind's eye?

◄◠ CROWN CHAKRA EXERCISE ◠►

Your crown chakra is your direct line to Cosmic Consciousness and the Divine. Practically speaking, it's ideal to work with the crown chakra when you need to view things from a different perspective. The energy of your crown chakra will help you detach from your worldly concerns and enable you to see struggles with a divine eye.

What current situation do you feel you might need to view from a different perspective?

···◆ AURAS ◆···

An aura is an energetic, electromagnetic field or atmosphere that surrounds all living things. Everyone's aura is different in size, shape, and color. Your aura says a lot about who you are and why you're here. Understanding your aura can offer insights around what challenges you may face in this life, your calling, and your physical, mental, and spiritual well-being.

The human aura is made up of seven layers, each with a distinct purpose and meaning. Your aura is one part of a more extensive system called the subtle energy body. The aura is given life through your chakra system. Similar to how your physical body systems work together, each of the subtle energy systems work together to make the whole function properly.

Your glowing aura is full of colors that can change throughout the day based on your mood and energy levels. Even though your aura colors can shift minute to minute, we are all born with one or two primary aura colors that stick with us throughout our lives. Your primary aura color is determined by your past lives, any karmic debt you might have brought into this lifetime, and your purpose during this lifetime.

Understanding the colors of your aura is a powerful and enlightening tool that will help you understand your purpose and path for this lifetime. Take in the following color descriptions as soft suggestions, not a definitive direction.

LAYERS OF THE AURA

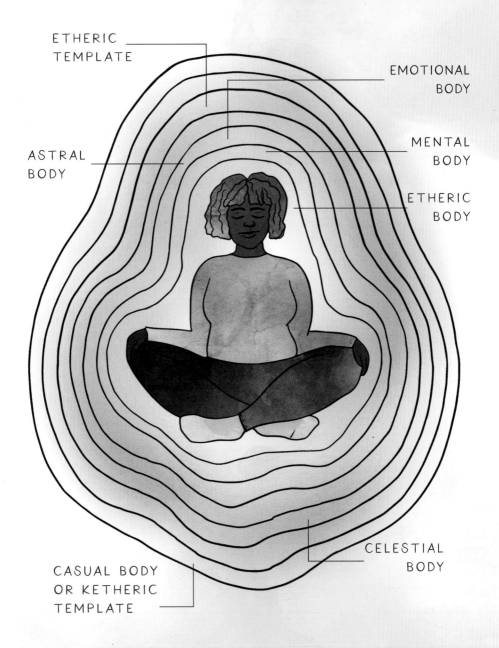

ETHERIC TEMPLATE

EMOTIONAL BODY

ASTRAL BODY

MENTAL BODY

ETHERIC BODY

CELESTIAL BODY

CASUAL BODY OR KETHERIC TEMPLATE

AURA COLORS AND THEIR MEANINGS

Most people have one or two primary aura colors that dominate their auric field. These colors, generally, stay with you throughout your lifetime. White and black are often seen as ancillary colors, not primary aura colors, but they are important, nonetheless.

YELLOW
Positive, energetic, driven, persistent

ORANGE
Vital, creative, adventurous, pleasure-driven

RED
Grounded, physical, passionate, quick to anger

PURPLE
Intuitive, perceptive, sensitive, introspective

BLUE
Calm, healing, natural teacher, communicative

GREEN
Optimistic, balanced, caring, patient

CRYSTAL
Empath, highly sensitive, compassionate, easily overwhelmed

WHITE
Deeply spiritual, virtuous, positive, disconnected from reality

BLACK
Power, magick, strength, blocked energy

UNDERSTANDING AND CONNECTING
WITH YOUR AURA

Auras are not generally visible to the naked eye. There can be colors, shapes, and patterns within auras, and these will all vary from person to person. Each aura is like a fingerprint, completely and totally unique. You can learn techniques to see them, but learning how to intuitively understand your auric field is the fastest and easiest route. Here are a few techniques to discover what colors are present in·your aura.

- **Connect with your chakras:** Quietly connect with each chakra. Which ones feel balanced and thriving, deficient, or overactive? The colors of your most active chakras will show up more in your auric field.

- **Ask to see the colors of your aura:** Close your eyes and ask for the colors of your aura to appear to you. Breathe and wait for colors to arise within your mind's eye. You may also receive a feeling or an inner knowing about what colors are present in your aura, and that's great, too. It's normal if nothing happens the first or second time you try. I suggest trying it a few times before you adopt a different method.

- **Feeling your aura:** Sitting down, take one to two minutes to connect with your breath and tune into your body. Rub your hands together for about thirty seconds. Begin to move your hands apart from each other slowly, then closer together, then apart again. You may begin to sense a tingling in your palms or light pressure in between your hands. Once you do, begin to hover your hands about two inches above your body. Pay attention to any sensations you feel in your hands or messages you receive.

- **Seeing your aura:** Begin rubbing your hands together for about thirty seconds. This time, instead of using your hands to feel your aura, you'll place your hands about six to eight inches apart from each other, about two feet from your face. Gently rest your eyes on the area in between your hands. Rather than focusing on the space in between your hands, try looking through that area, as if there's a screen in between your hands that you're trying to look through.

The first part of the aura that usually appears is the etheric layer, because it is the densest layer of the aura. The etheric layer will usually show up as white, gray, or very light blue. If you're seeing a faint haze of any of these colors in the area between your hands, you're seeing the first layer of your aura!

·•◇ AURA QUIZ ◁•·

Check each statement that resonates with you. Tally the total for each color. The colors that have the highest numbers are the most prominent ones that make up your aura at this moment in your life. Though I don't recommend using a quiz like this as your only method to connect with your aura, it can be a fun tool to cross-reference what you sensed with your intuition.

·◁〰 YELLOW 〰▷·

☐ I consider myself a lifelong learner.

☐ I need to see the results of my work.

☐ I am optimistic.

☐ My willpower is strong.

☐ I consider myself a healthy person.

Total: _____

◄ ORANGE ►

- ☐ I enjoy a good adventure.
- ☐ I am a thrill seeker.
- ☐ I enjoy creative activities.
- ☐ I make having pleasurable experiences a priority.
- ☐ I think play is essential.

Total: _____

◄ RED ►

- ☐ I enjoy physical activities.
- ☐ I enjoy physical touch.
- ☐ I consider myself a very sensual and sexually expressive person.
- ☐ I am sometimes quick to anger.
- ☐ I find it difficult to imagine things that I cannot see.

Total: _____

◄ PURPLE ►

- ☐ I can see situations from multiple perspectives.
- ☐ I feel called to help humanity and the planet.
- ☐ I am sensitive to other people's energy.
- ☐ I am very intuitive.
- ☐ Sometimes I feel like I don't belong here.

Total: _____

BLUE

- ☐ I consider myself an advocate for social justice.
- ☐ I consider myself a leader and a teacher.
- ☐ Public speaking doesn't scare me.
- ☐ I am intuitive.
- ☐ I love to have discussions with people.

Total: _____

GREEN

- ☐ I am very organized.
- ☐ I enjoy the outdoors and connecting with nature.
- ☐ The well-being of others is important to me.
- ☐ I enjoy being of service to others.
- ☐ I make money easily.

Total: _____

CRYSTAL

- ☐ I can easily sense people's emotions.
- ☐ Rooms full of people feel overwhelming to me.
- ☐ I try to lift people up when I'm around them.
- ☐ I can become easily overwhelmed by other people's emotions.
- ☐ Time by myself is important to my well-being.

Total: _____

Based on the aura quiz and any other intuition techniques, how does your aura color align with your personality or your current circumstances? If it doesn't, in what ways does it differ?

When do you feel like you need the most energetic protection?
Around certain people? Specific places?

The next time you're around a person or in a place where you feel energetically vulnerable, pause and visualize your aura expanding outward and providing you with a protective field of energy. How did it feel to do this? Did it work better around specific people or in specific places?

···◈ THE FOUR ELEMENTS ◈···

The four elements—earth, air, water, and fire—make up the Universe. They are in you and all around you and manifest in both physical and energetic ways. The four elements go beyond passive energies and can each be called upon to shift your energy and your space. They are foundational for understanding natural magick and the energetic world. As you already learned in the chakra section, each energy center corresponds with one of these elements. Understanding the elements will help you better understand your energy and be able to shift it when needed.

EACH ELEMENT CARRIES ITS OWN SET OF QUALITIES. NO ELEMENT IS INHERENTLY BAD OR GOOD. THEY EACH CARRY AN EQUAL AMOUNT OF POSITIVE AND NEGATIVE TRAITS.

The elements are here to bring balance, both physically and energetically. In nature, fire needs water to be quenched, and the earth needs air to move and grow. The elements are reflected in your personality as well. For example, you might consider yourself very fiery or have a lot of fire in your astrological birth chart (which we'll explore in the astrology section!), and this plays a role in how you express yourself. The elements of your personality can be balanced just like nature. If you're a very fiery person and need to balance it out, you can add slower and softer routines associated with the element of water, like taking a bath.

FIRE

To stimulate fire energy, you can exercise, light candles, plan an adventure, or practice a solar plexus chakra meditation.

Strengths: Courageous, intense, passionate
Weaknesses: Angry, obsessive, jealous
Chakra: Solar plexus chakra
Direction: South
Colors: Orange, red

AIR

To stimulate more air energy, you can spend more time outside, activate the throat by singing or yelling, have conversations with others, start a new project, or do a heart or throat chakra meditation.

Strengths: Communicative, analytical, imaginative
Weaknesses: Overthinking, dishonest, flaky
Chakras: Heart and throat chakras
Direction: East
Color: Yellow

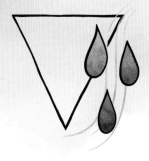

WATER

If you need to incorporate more water energy in your life, you can take a bath or shower, dance, drink more water, get creative, or do a sacral chakra meditation.

Strengths: Healing, intuitive, creative
Weaknesses: Overly emotional, depressive, erratic
Chakra: Sacral chakra
Direction: West
Color: Blue

EARTH

If you need to connect to earth energy, you can spend more time in nature, garden, add plants to your living space, eat warm and hearty foods, or do a root chakra meditation.

Strengths: Grounded, logical, nurturing
Weaknesses: Lazy, stubborn, materialistic
Chakra: Root chakra
Direction: North
Colors: Green, black

◄◝ HOW TO USE THE FOUR ELEMENTS ◝►

Understanding your personality: What are your strengths and weaknesses based on the information on pages 31 to 32? You can use this information to lean into the elements that manifest more naturally within you by choosing careers, activities, and relationships that play to your strengths.

Balancing your energy: Being able to shift your energy with the four elements is a powerful way to feel more balanced. For example, if you know that you lean toward airy energy and are experiencing a lot of anxiety, building in extra time to connect with the earth will help you feel more stable and grounded.

Ritual and magick: The four elements are foundational in natural magick. They can be used individually for spellwork and ritual to call upon a specific kind of energy or collectively for powerful energetic protection. See page 54 for a ritual on energy protection using the four elements!

Which element seems to fit your personality? In what ways?

Which element(s) do you feel an aversion to? In what ways?

·•◊ WATER ELEMENT ◊•·

Go for a swim, or take a bath or a shower, then set some time and write down what comes to mind at that moment. What lessons does water have to teach you?

·•◇ EARTH ELEMENT ◁•·

Take a moment to go outside for a walk, or if you can't go outside, take a moment to close your eyes and visualize being outside in your favorite natural environment. Does the natural environment you're in provide any insights or wisdom?

·•◇ AIR ELEMENT ◁•·

Take time to express yourself vocally. Sing, yell, laugh, talk, or make any sounds you feel called to. Allow yourself to do this for as long as you want to, and try not to judge what comes out of your mouth. How did performing this activity make you feel as you were doing it?

·•◊ FIRE ELEMENT ◊•·

Light a candle and stay with it as it burns. Close your eyes and visualize this flame at your solar plexus or core area. Visualize it growing in intensity and heat. Stay with this visualization for five to ten breaths or longer if you like. How does your body feel after connecting with the flame and visualizing the fire within you?

···◆ ASTROLOGY ◆···

Your astrological birth chart is a snapshot of the sky at your birth. Each planet and zodiac sign carry different energies. When you arrive earthside, the location of these different energies has an effect on you and imbues you with certain dispositions, challenges, and purpose. However, it's important to state that your birth chart is not your fate. You always have free will. Think of your birth chart as a flexible map with gentle suggestions. Understanding your birth chart can offer deep insight into your purpose for being here, and it can also help you make more sense of your challenges.

Astrology is a massive field of study. There are even different kinds of astrology! Everything in this section will be explained through the lens of Western or Tropical astrology. My goal here is to give you a basic understanding of what your birth chart is, and an understanding of the twelve zodiac signs, planets, and houses, and their energetic correspondences. Understanding these basic areas will give you the tools you need to better understand your energy from an astrological perspective.

·◁◡ YOUR BIRTH CHART ◡▷·

A few factors play into your birth chart—the time of your birth, the day you were born, and the location where you were born. For an accurate birth chart, you'll need all three of these pieces of information. If you are unable to determine your birth time, you can still have a chart created and learn your Sun sign, and know where the planets were the day you were born. You can usually determine your Moon sign too, but the Moon does cycle through signs relatively quickly, so this may not be exact. Without your birth time, you won't be able to determine your Rising sign or have an accurate look at your houses.

To acquire a birth chart, using this information, do an online search, in any search engine, for a "free birth chart." Several options will be available.

◂◝ YOUR SUN, MOON, AND RISING SIGNS ◝▸

The most common sign people know is their Sun sign, but this is just one small part of your birth chart! That said, your Sun sign is still important and part of what many astrologers call your "big three." Your big three is your Sun, Moon, and Rising signs, and they have the biggest influence over your personality, subconscious, and purpose.

♦ **Sun sign:** Relates to your ego and the way in which you express yourself

♦ **Moon sign:** Relates to your subconscious and how you experience your emotional world

♦ **Rising sign:** Relates to who you are and what you bring to the world

·•◊ TIP ◁•·

Drawing your birth chart can be a creative way to learn the anatomy of your chart. Find a free fillable version at *cassieuhl.com/diy-birth-chart*

BIRTH CHART

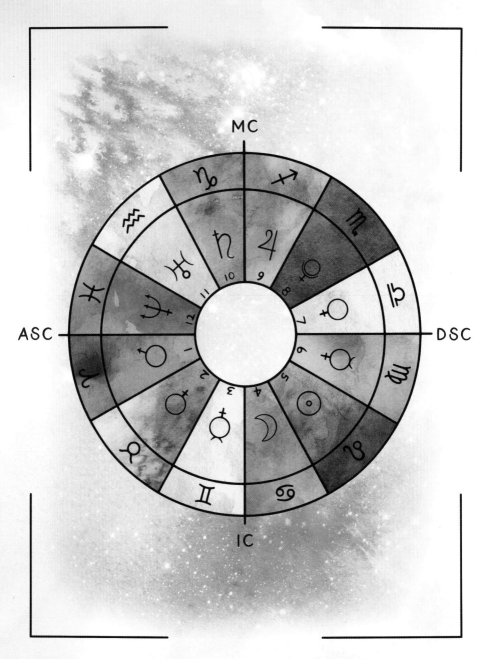

MC

ASC

DSC

IC

42

ARIES

Dates: March 21–April 19
Element: Fire
Traits: Action-oriented, passionate, energetic, impatient, discontent

TAURUS

Dates: April 20–May 20
Element: Earth
Traits: Pleasure-oriented, physical, reliable, stubborn, opinionated

GEMINI

Dates: May 21–June 21
Element: Air
Traits: Communicative, friendly, charming, temperamental, gossipy

CANCER

Dates: June 22–July 22
Element: Water
Traits: Family-oriented, sensitive, empathetic, possessive, guarded

LEO

Dates: July 23–August 22
Element: Fire
Traits: Joyful, extroverted, heart-centered, narcissistic, overbearing

VIRGO

Dates: August 23–September 22
Element: Earth
Traits: Analytical, nurturing, service-oriented, perfectionist, restrained

LIBRA

Dates: September 23–October 22

Element: Air

Traits: Peaceful, reciprocal, idealistic, codependent, indecisive

SCORPIO

Dates: October 23–November 22

Element: Water

Traits: Honest, insightful, intense, demanding, destructive

SAGITTARIUS

Dates: November 23–December 21

Element: Fire

Traits: Truthful, adventurous, independent, excessive, rash

CAPRICORN

Dates: December 22–January 19

Element: Earth

Traits: Persistent, persevering, structured, authoritarian, materialistic

AQUARIUS

Dates: January 20–February 18

Element: Air

Traits: Outspoken, authentic, humanitarian, stubborn, rebellious

PISCES

Dates: February 19–March 20

Element: Water

Traits: Intuitive, spiritual, dreamy, unrealistic, addiction-prone

SUN
The Ego

MOON
The
Subconscious

MERCURY
Communication
Style

VENUS
Love

MARS
Power

JUPITER
Areas of
Expansion

SATURN
Structure

URANUS
Eccentricities

NEPTUNE
Dreams

PLUTO
Transformations

✦◡ ASTROLOGICAL HOUSES ◡✦

1ST HOUSE
Identity +
appearance

2ND HOUSE
Money +
materiality

3RD HOUSE
Communication +
learning

4TH HOUSE
Family +
security

5TH HOUSE
Romance +
play

6TH HOUSE
Service +
health

7TH HOUSE
Relationships +
marriage

8TH HOUSE
Birth, death +
transformation

9TH HOUSE
Travel +
expansion

10TH HOUSE
Career +
purpose

11TH HOUSE
Friendships +
social justice

12TH HOUSE
Imagination +
dreams

Which parts of your personality make more sense after exploring your Sun, Moon, and Rising signs?

What were you surprised to learn about yourself after exploring your Sun, Moon, and Rising signs?

Write down which houses have the highest concentration of planets on your birth chart. How do you feel about the areas of life in which you have the most houses?

Write down which zodiac signs have the highest concentration of planets on your birth chart. How do you feel like these signs influence your personality?

···◆ PROTECTION RITUALS ◆···

While getting to know your chakras, auras, and subtle energy system, and fine-tuning your psychic abilities, it's important to properly protect your energy body from negative energy or energy vampires. If you're a highly sensitive person, you will benefit from daily protection rituals. You can perform protection rituals whenever you feel they are needed, regardless of whether you are performing other spiritual work. Protection rituals are great to perform while you're doing psychic work like tarot card readings or performing spells or rituals.

Let's go through a couple of these methods that will keep you protected.

◄◡ PROTECTIVE CRYSTALS ◡►

Crystals are a great way to keep yourself protected. There are a variety of crystals available that can offer protection. Black tourmaline, hematite, labradorite, and amethyst are ideal crystals for energetic protection. To use them in this way, consider carrying them in your pocket, wearing them, or placing them around your living space.

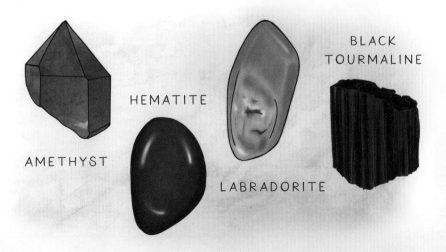

BLACK TOURMALINE

HEMATITE

AMETHYST

LABRADORITE

◦◦ AFFIRMATIONS FOR PROTECTION ◦◦

Your words are powerful and can be used as spells. Try reciting some of these affirmations in your mind or aloud anytime you want to feel safer, grounded, or protected. Add "so it is" or "so mote it be" after the affirmation, if you feel called.

···～···

AS I STAND, I FEEL THE EARTH UNDER MY FEET
AND KNOW I AM PROTECTED AND HELD.

···～···

MY AURA IS WHOLE AND GLOWING. IT EXPANDS
WITH EACH BREATH THAT I TAKE.

···～···

ANY NEGATIVE ENERGY DIRECTED AT ME WILL
NOT AFFECT ME AND WILL BE REFLECTED BACK
TO THE SENDER.

···～···

⊰∿ ALGIZ RUNE FOR PROTECTION ∿⊱

Runes are symbols that each carry unique universal energy. These special symbols were used by Nordic and Germanic cultures in Northern Europe as forms of language, for religious purposes, and as tools of magick and divination.

The Algiz Rune carries the energy of a protective spirit guide, always watching over you. This Rune offers both protection and guidance on your journey. Tap into the power of Algiz anytime you need additional protection or feel like you don't know how to move forward in your life. Here are three ways to call on the Algiz Rune for protection.

- ◆ Consider drawing the Algiz Rune in areas or on items that you'd like to protect.

- ◆ Create an Algiz Rune shape from tree branches to place in your home or above your bed as a sign of protection.

- ◆ Combine salt and water to make a salt water solution. Dip your finger in the solution and draw the Algiz Rune on walls, floors, or windows where you'd like more protection.

◄～ CALLING THE QUARTERS FOR PROTECTION ～►

The cardinal directions—North, South, East, and West—can help you with more than navigation. Each direction can be "called on" as a tool for protection during ritual. Each direction coordinates with one of the four elements (earth, air, water, and fire). By calling on the quarters for protection, you're also invoking the four elements as protective forces.

This method of protection is called "calling the quarters." Beyond protection, this technique also creates a sacred space that is connected to the spirit realm. There's more than one way to call the quarters. A quick internet search will offer you a variety of options, but here's one way:

Imagine each direction as a wind that you're beckoning into your space. You can even imagine a specific Goddess or God representing the wind of each. Face the direction of each quarter as you call them, and ask each to join you for your ritual or magick work. Many like to start by calling in the North wind first because it will keep your ritual grounded. When you're done performing your ritual work, release the winds, and thank them for their assistance and protection.

The next time you perform a spell, practice a ritual, or want to tune into your intuition, practice the "calling the quarters" protection ritual on page 54. After performing the ritual, how did you feel? Did you notice a shift in the energy around you, and if so, how?

Write a list of people, places, and things that you feel energetically drained by.

What kind of boundaries could you put in place to feel better protected from these things?

If the boundaries you'd ideally want to put in place are not possible, which of the previous tools could you start using to feel better supported around these people, places, and things?

After implementing some tools to better support yourself around energy draining people, places, or things, how do you feel?

CHAPTER 2

INTUITION

Intuition is the quiet internal voice or feeling to trust someone or not, leave a space, or take a leap on a new journey or life path. Our intuitive voice can be easily drowned out by the to-dos of the mundane world and our very natural fears. The good news is that your intuition is just like a muscle—exercise it regularly and you'll soon discover your intuitive superpowers and become more and more comfortable with recognizing your unique intuitive voice.

YOUR INTUITION IS YOUR INTERNAL COMPASS THAT'S DEDICATED TO LEADING YOU TO YOUR SOUL'S DEEPEST DESIRES.

Every human comes into this world with natural intuitive abilities. However, we all experience our intuitive abilities differently. In this section, you'll learn ways to better understand your intuition and the tools that will best serve you. You don't need tools to use your intuition, but they can be an incredibly helpful ally, especially when you are just beginning. There are countless tools to begin experimenting with your intuitive abilities, like tarot and oracle cards, palmistry, Runes, and even numerology. Some of these techniques have more guidelines than others, but they're all enhanced by having a solid understanding of how your intuitive voice speaks.

·••◆ TUNE INTO YOUR INTUITION ◆••·

There are several ways to tune into your intuition and listen to what it might be telling you. In this section, you'll learn how to identify what your natural intuitive abilities are and ways to start using them. There are five primary methods for receiving intuitive information and they're called the clairs.

Think of the clairs as ways that intuitive information can come through your body. These are modes of communication for psychic information and the intuition. Most people have one or two clairs that are the primary ways they receive intuitive or psychic information. Regardless of what your strengths are, all of the clairs can be learned and honed over time. Here's more information about each clair.

- ◆ **Clairvoyance or Clear Seeing:** You are likely to see apparitions or spirits, see visions in your mind's eye, and are likely a very visual person.

- ◆ **Clairaudience or Clear Hearing:** You might hear sounds or voices within the mind that come through as messages, or even voices that seem to come from outside of you.

- ◆ **Clairsentience or Clear Feeling:** You feel the energy of the room when you walk into it or can tell when someone is happy or sad just by standing next to them.

- ◆ **Clairtangency or Clear Touching:** You receive information or intuitive hits about people or places through touch.

- ◆ **Claircognizance or Clear Knowing:** You tend to know things without any explanation and may experience insights through your dreams.

◁⌣ WAYS TO INSPIRE YOUR INTUITION ⌣▷

Here are five easy ways to begin opening up to your intuition. I encourage you to give them all a try to better understand which ones you enjoy the most.

♦ **Quiet your mind regularly:** Regular meditation or quiet reflection are essential to tuning in to your intuition. Try setting aside a minimum of five minutes every day to sit in silence and focus on your breath and body.

♦ **Ask for signs:** Ask your intuition for clear signs. Be specific! Rather than asking, "Show me a sign," try, "Show me a feather today if I'm on the right path."

♦ **Focus on your third eye:** Your third eye is an energy center connected to your pineal gland. Try focusing on the third eye, located in between the brow bones, as you meditate or use intuitive tools.

♦ **Intuitive tools:** Using tools to interpret and better understand intuitive messages is a great way to become more comfortable with your intuition. See page 61 for examples of some tools you can use, which are also covered further in this chapter.

What fears do you have about trusting your intuition? Have any of these fears come true? If so, how did it make you feel?

Write about a time when you trusted your intuition. What was it trying to tell you?

Write about a time when you didn't listen to your intuition. What did you learn from this experience?

What intuitive tool do you feel the most drawn to, and what about it is most appealing?

*How would you like to use your intuitive abilities to help yourself
and to help others?*

Think about a time when you felt anxious. What did it feel like in your body and mind? How do your feelings of anxiety differ from your intuition?

⋯◆ ORACLE AND TAROT CARDS ◆⋯

Whenever you're seeking guidance in a particular area of your life, oracle and tarot cards can help. The best thing about using cards to access your intuitive abilities is how diverse they are. Tarot and oracle cards can be used to provide a little wisdom for the day, messages from spirits or guides, or insights into significant life challenges.

In this section, you'll explore a deck of tarot or oracle cards, to get more comfortable with your intuition. You'll learn more about different kinds of card spreads and how to perform readings for yourself and others. Before we dive in, let's explore some of the similarities and differences between tarot and oracle cards.

◄◡ ORACLE CARDS ◡►

♦ Can have any number of cards.

♦ Do not follow a set structure.

♦ Usually based around a theme.

♦ Card meanings usually have more room for personal interpretation.

♦ Learning card meanings will be different for each deck.

◄◡ TAROT CARDS ◡►

♦ A deck has 78 cards consisting of 22 Major and 56 Minor Arcana.

♦ The Minor Arcana is broken into four suits, usually wands, swords, pentacles, and cups.

♦ Artwork will differ but the names of the cards remain the same among most tarot decks.

♦ Once you understand the card meanings for one tarot deck you will be able to read almost any tarot deck.

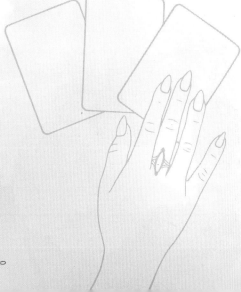

Your oracle and tarot cards can collect energy from other people, yourself, and your environment. There are several things you can do to keep your decks energetically fresh so that you receive and give the best readings. It's a good idea to cleanse your cards when you receive a new deck, let someone else handle them, or if they have been sitting for a long time without use.

Cleanse the cards with herbal smoke, salt, or sunlight by holding them in your hands and calling on cleansing energy from the spirit realm, or any other cleansing methods you prefer.

HOW TO PERFORM A CARD READING

These are suggested steps to perform a card reading for yourself or others with a tarot or an oracle card deck.

1. Go within for a few breaths to quiet your mind. Decide on a topic for your reading.

2. *Optional:* Invite any guides or helping spirits into the reading to help you.

3. Decide how many cards you'd like to pull for your card spread. Consider writing your questions down beforehand to help you stay on topic as you perform your reading.

4. Holding your deck in your hands, focus intently on your question. Shuffle your cards until you feel called to stop. Select all of the cards for your spread from the top of the deck or reshuffle for each card. Alternatively, slide your cards out in a line and hover your hand over them until you feel called to select a card.

5. Pull your card(s) and lay them out in front of you. Try not to judge them and what they mean to you. Things will make more sense once you've pulled out all of your cards.

6. Start deciphering your card message. Take in all of the cards at once. Notice what designs, colors, and words stand out to you the most. Notice the order of the cards and how they flow together, and perhaps even tell a story. Feel free to explore any guidebooks you have as additional references.

7. Thank your cards and any helpers you called on for the reading. Consider journaling about your reading for deeper insights.

Here are a few card spreads you can try to find guidance on your path forward. Remember, the cards can help lead you, but don't expect definitive answers. Think of your card readings as soft suggestions and ways to help navigate your current experiences and emotions.

·●◊ ONE-CARD PULL ◊●·

Have a question and not much time? Close your eyes, focus intently on your question, then ask your intuition to answer you through your deck of choice. Invite the wisdom of the card into your day and notice how your relationship with it unfolds throughout your day.

·●◊ THREE-CARD SPREAD ◊●·

A three-card spread works well for specific situations that you're seeking clarity on. The three cards can have a variety of meanings depending on the kind of question you asked.

- ◆ **Card 1:** Past, Problem, Mind

- ◆ **Card 2:** Present, Solution, Body

- ◆ **Card 3:** Future, Outcome, Spirit

·✦◟ FIVE-CARD COMPASS SPREAD ◞✦·

Dig deep into the big picture and overall direction of your life with this five-card compass spread.

♦ **Card 1:** Where you are presently.

♦ **Card 2:** Upcoming challenges.

♦ **Card 3:** Things to consider before moving forward.

♦ **Card 4:** What is the next step moving forward?

♦ **Card 5:** Your potential.

What situation or experience do you feel most called to explore with your cards? How do you feel about this situation or experience right now?

After pulling your cards, spend two to three minutes taking in all of the cards. What are the first three things that stood out to you about the cards you pulled? How did these three things make you feel?

Now notice the order of your cards. Do you see any themes or stories that the order of them seems to share? If so, how might these themes or stories apply to your situation?

_____

_____

_____

_____

_____

_____

_____

_____

_____

_____

_____

_____

_____

_____

What insights have you gained from this card spread and how can you apply some of this information to your life right now?

···◇ PALMISTRY ◇···

Palmistry, or chiromancy, is rooted in thousands of years of practice. It has been passed down from generation to generation, surviving major suppression by leaders such as King Henry VIII, who outlawed the practice along with astrology. From India, palm reading spread to China, where it remains closely linked with Chinese medicine and astrology. Today, palm reading is practiced all over the world.

This section is designed as an overview to get you started reading palms. You'll learn about the major and minor lines of the hand.

CHANGING YOURSELF FOR THE BETTER CAN BE DIFFICULT, BUT IT IS ALWAYS WORTHWHILE.

Many palmists believe that the lines on your hand can change over time. If you see something on your hand or someone else's hand that seems negative or scary, remember, you may not know the full picture, and nothing is set in stone, not even the lines on your hands!

Let's begin with the most important lines on your hand, the three major lines.

·•◊ TIP ◊•·

It's standard for the dominant hand to be used for a reading. The nondominant hand does have meaning, but the dominant hand has the most relevant information and is the best place to start.

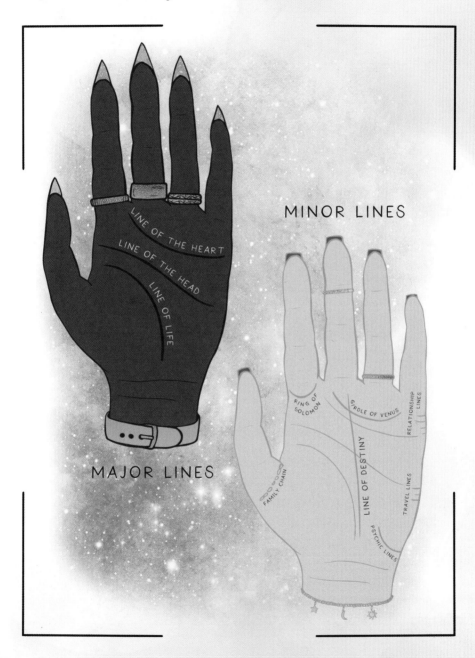

LINE OF THE HEART

LINE OF THE HEAD

LINE OF LIFE

MAJOR LINES

MINOR LINES

RING OF SOLOMON

GIRDLE OF VENUS

RELATIONSHIP LINES

LINE OF DESTINY

FAMILY CHAIN

TRAVEL LINES

PSYCHIC LINES

◂〜 THE MAJOR LINES 〜▸

The three major lines are the deepest and most dominant lines on your hand. The lines of the heart, head, and life each tell a unique story about you.

·•◊ LINE OF THE HEART ◁•·

The heart line, sometimes called the love line, can help shed light on your emotional energy, physical love, and the health of your heart. This line also connects deeply to your soul. A clear and deep heart line indicates that you will have a stable emotional life. A straight heart line indicates that you are more sensitive. If your heart line curves more, it indicates that you are more expressive with your emotions.

·•◊ LINE OF THE HEAD ◁•·

The head line is related to your intellect and how you use your mind. The length and depth of your head line is not directly related to your intelligence. Instead, this line reveals information about the way you think. The longer and deeper the head line is, the more intricate your thinking process is. A straight head line reveals that you are logical. A curved line indicates that you are imaginative.

·•◊ LINE OF LIFE ◁•·

The life line starts on the thumb side of the hand under the head line. Your life line reveals information about your energy and stamina levels over the course of your life. The life line is not a representation of how long or short your life will be. Long, deep lines reflect that you'll experience an abundance of vitality in your life. If your life line reaches farther into the middle of your hand it indicates that you'll have more energy throughout your life, while a life line that hugs closer to the thumb indicates lower energy.

◁〜 THE MINOR LINES 〜▷

Most of the remaining lines on your hand are minor lines. Most people's hands do not have every single minor line, and the lines that do appear may be very faint. In rare instances, some people have no minor lines. Everyone is different.

·•◊ GIRDLE OF VENUS ◁•·

This line often indicates that you're very sensitive and emotional.

·•◊ RING OF SOLOMON ◁•·

If you have a ring of Solomon line you likely rely heavily on your intuition and love all things spirituality.

·•◊ LINE OF DESTINY ◁•·

A strong, deep line of destiny represents the potential for a successful career.

·•◊ FAMILY CHAIN ◁•·

Your family chain reveals how close you'll be with your family over time. Strong and bold links indicate times of closeness and lighter and disconnected links indicate times of limited contact with your family.

·•◊ RELATIONSHIP LINES ◁•·

Sometimes called "marriage lines," these fine lines represent how many meaningful relationships you may have over the course of your life.

·•◊ PSYCHIC LINE ◁•·

As the name suggests, a strong psychic line means you likely have a natural ability for connecting with the spirit world.

·•◊ TRAVEL LINES ◁•·

Travel lines indicate longer and momentous trips.

After exploring your palm, what makes the most sense and what surprised you the most?

Did any parts of exploring your palm inspire your intuition?

In what ways could you lean into your intuition more
while performing palm readings?

Are there any parts of your palm that make you question your current path? If so, how? If not, in what ways did exploring your palm encourage you to stay on your current path?

After looking at your heart line, does it feel like an accurate representation of your emotional energy? Why? Or why not?

Does your head line indicate that you are a more logical or creative person? Does this feel like an accurate representation of you? How so? Or how not?

NUMEROLOGY

Numbers are the language of the Universe and they cannot lie, no matter your background or faith—two plus two will always equal four. Numbers connect all of us, not only with each other but also with nature and the entire Universe. Each number carries a vibration of energy. Similar to other intuitive tools, numerology has suggested meanings and uses. Your intuition comes through in the way that you interpret and apply numeric meanings and messages to your life.

You'll learn how to determine your life path number and basic number meanings. The numbers used in numerology are one to nine, because all other numbers can be made from these. There are also a few "master numbers" used by most numerologists, including numbers eleven, twenty-two, and thirty-three.

TIP

See repeating numbers often? These are often called angel numbers and may be signs from a spirit guide or angel trying to get your attention. You can apply the number meanings on pages 92 and 93 to your numeric message to gain more insight into the numeric messages you see.

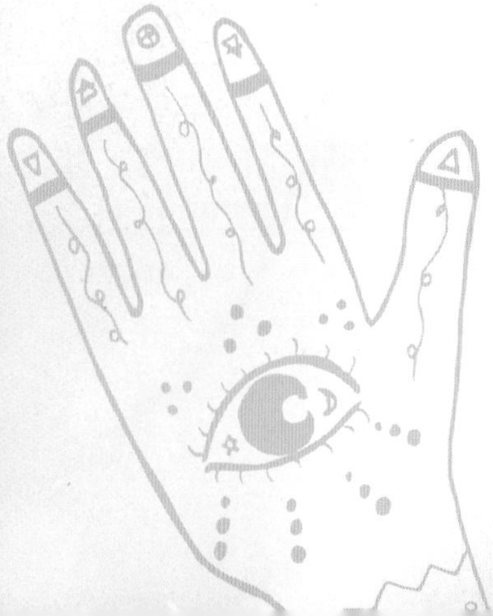

DETERMINING YOUR LIFE PATH NUMBER

Your life path number is determined by your birth date. Each number is added up until you end with a single digit between one and nine, or a master number (eleven, twenty-two, or thirty-three). Here's how to determine your life path number with your birth date.

1. Add your birth month together if it is two digits. For example, if your birth month is November, you'll add 1+1 to get two, but if it is March, you will keep it as a three.

2. Add your birth date together if it is two digits. For example, if you were born on the twenty-fourth day of the month you will add together 2+4 to get six.

3. Add your birth year numbers together. For example, if you were born in 1999 you will add 1+9+9+9 to get twenty-eight, then add 2+8 to get ten, then add 1+0 to arrive at one.

4. When you have your three single digits you will add all three together. If they equal a double digit that isn't a master number, you will add them together again until they are a single digit or a master number.

Your life path number can give you insight into your purpose for being here. Explore the meaning of your life path number below.

1 Independent ones love to go at it alone. Careers that will allow you to make your own decisions and be in charge are ideal.

2 Cooperative twos feel most at ease in a pair. You thrive in happy and healthy relationships with friends, and having a solid partner is very important to your well-being.

3 Creative threes feel most alive putting on a show for others. You most likely have a creative gift of some kind, whether it be in the visual arts, performance, or written, and you love to share your gifts.

4 Dedicated fours are committed to accomplishing their goals. You're a hard worker and never give up on a challenge. You have a strong ability to think through problems with logic and innovation.

5 Active fives are charismatic busybodies. Change doesn't frighten you at all. In fact, you thrive off of it! You probably find yourself the life of the party in many situations.

6 Nurturing sixes are natural caregivers. You probably find that you're the person friends come to in a time of need. That's because your life path is to care for others and give.

7 Contemplative sevens are on a mission to uncover the truth. You're intrigued by universal unknowns and likely feel a strong pull to find solutions to big life quandaries.

8 Master manifesting eights have powerful minds and an even stronger will. Be careful what you wish for! Your ability to create your own reality is stronger than most.

9 Empathic nines are generous humanitarians. You feel the pain of others and the world and desperately want to fix it. Your loved ones likely find you very trustworthy and honest.

11 Inspiring elevens are natural-born teachers. You are here on this Earth to carry inspiring messages to your fellow humans. Though this may seem like a daunting task, it is your purpose for being here.

22 Master builder twenty-twos can turn their visions into reality with ease. You are a perfect combination of spiritual and grounded. You excel at seeing the big picture and finding balance.

33 Master healer thirty-threes are the ultimate creative healers. You care deeply about the well-being of others and the world. Having the double energy of the three, you are extremely artistic and creative.

What are your initial thoughts about your life path number? Does it make sense to you or does it seem a little off—if so, how?

After reading about your life path number, how do you think you could be in better alignment with your life path or calling? What actions could you take?

What fears do you have around making changes in your life to feel more aligned with your path and desires?

Write about one small change you could make in your life to start moving toward something you feel called to explore.

What numbers do you feel particularly drawn to or see often?

How do those numbers make you feel when you see them, and do the meanings of them shared in this section match?

···◆ RUNES ◆···

Runes are rooted in Old Norse history and make up an ancient alphabet containing twenty-four symbols. Each Runic symbol has a meaning and a story of its own. They have been discovered on spearheads, charms, and even on headstones in the form of spells. The word *Rune* has come to mean "secret" or "something hidden."

Runes are diverse tools. They can be used for divination purposes and as magickal tools. Similar to oracle and tarot cards, a set of Rune tiles can be used for daily guidance or insights around larger life events. For this section, we'll focus on using Runes as an intuitive tool.

There are a couple of common ways to use your Runes as an intuitive tool. You can select Runes by hand, similar to an oracle or a tarot card reading, or cast all twenty-four Runes for a full reading—reading Runes in this way will take practice and familiarity with the Runes themselves. For a simple Rune reading, craft your own set of Rune tiles (outlined on page 104), and intuitively select some Runes just as you would a tarot or an oracle card.

◁〰 RUNE MEANINGS 〰▷

Each Rune has a lengthy history and meaning—these suggestions are just a starting point. If you feel called to working with Runes, I encourage you to explore their meanings even further.

FEHU
Abundance, Prosperity

URUZ
Strength, Health

THURISAZ
Empowerment, Defense

ANSUZ
Communication, Signs

RAIDHO
Journey, Initiative

KAUNAZ
Creativity, Transformation

GEBO
Gratitude, Partnership

WUNJU
Joy, Harmony

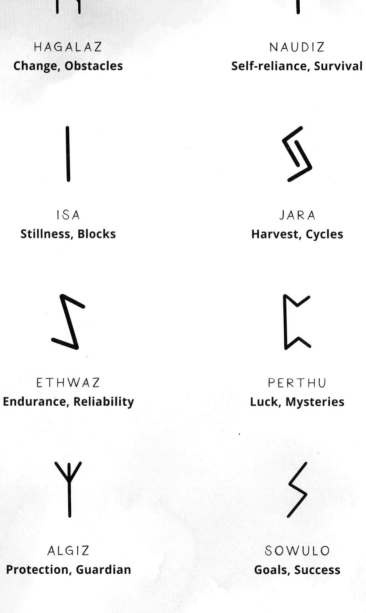

HAGALAZ
Change, Obstacles

NAUDIZ
Self-reliance, Survival

ISA
Stillness, Blocks

JARA
Harvest, Cycles

ETHWAZ
Endurance, Reliability

PERTHU
Luck, Mysteries

ALGIZ
Protection, Guardian

SOWULO
Goals, Success

TEIWAS
Spiritual Warrior, Leadership

BERKANA
Growth, Rebirth

EHWAZ
Teamwork, Trust

MANNAZ
The Self, Awareness

LAGUZ
Flow, Renewal

INGWAZ
Wholeness, Home

DAGAZ
Enlightenment, Breakthrough

OTHALA
Inheritance, Freedom

CREATE YOUR OWN RUNE TILES

Rune tiles can easily be purchased online or at a local witchy or metaphysical supply store, but making your own can be really special and allows you to begin forming a relationship with each Rune. Plus, Rune tiles are easy to make and you can always upgrade your set later.

You'll need:

♦ 24 pieces of paper, wood, or stone for your Rune tiles

♦ Paint or permanent marker to draw your Runes

♦ The Rune guide from this journal

Instructions:

1. With your materials at hand, spend two to five minutes creating a sacred space. Close your eyes and connect with your breath and body. Consider calling on any ancestors or spirit guides to be present as you create your tiles.

2. Using the Rune guide in this book as your reference, draw or paint each Rune onto paper, wood, or stone.

3. As you draw or paint each symbol, focus intently on the shape of each Rune and its meaning. This will help you begin to form a connection with each Rune.

4. Once you're done, consider holding a little ceremony for your new Rune tiles. You can pass them through some cleansing smoke, bless them with your hands, or recite some meaningful words.

What stood out to you the most from your Rune readings? Which parts made the most sense to you? Which parts left you with more questions?

Which Rune symbol stood out to you the most initially? What do you like about it? How does the meaning of this Rune connect with you and your life right now?

Which Rune symbol do you dislike the most? What do you dislike about it?
Where do you think this aversion stems from?

CHAPTER 3

MAGICK AND
SPELLWORK

Now that you've explored your energy and discovered ways to lean into your intuition, it's time to learn tools to help you more intentionally direct your energy and enhance your intuition. Both magick and spellwork are ways to combine specific tools and intentions at specific times to help bring about a desired outcome. There are endless ways to do this and in this section you'll learn some of the most common tools used in spellwork and magick, such as herbs, plants, Moon phases, crystals, and timing.

When working with magick and spellwork you'll be dealing with correspondences, which are items, symbols, and times that match energy and complement each other. When you combine items that correspond with each other you increase the energy of your desired outcome; combine this with your own visualizations and intentions and you've got a powerful way to shift energy.

SPELLWORK AND MAGICK ETHICS

We can't talk about spellwork and magick without discussing ethics. Many in the Pagan and Witchcraft world honor the "rule of three," which is the belief that any harmful magick or spells you put out into the world will come back to you three-fold. Based on this premise, I generally do not recommend performing harmful spells. Secondly, we all have free will, which means it isn't advised to perform spells or magick with the goal of changing someone's mind or an outcome that involves another person. This is a topic that comes up often with love spells. Something to consider instead is, how can you shift your own energy to better receive a loving relationship, rather than forcing someone to love you?

⋯•◇ HERBS AND PLANTS ◇•⋯

Even if you are incapable of keeping a houseplant alive, you can still enjoy the magickal properties of plants and herbs. Plants and herbs are endowed with both healing and magickal properties. Use plants to cleanse the energy of your space, offer protection during psychic work, or encourage more abundance. Whatever your need, there's almost certainly a plant that can help.

Plants have existed far longer than humans. In fact, they're one of the oldest magickal tools in existence, making their benefits both varied and powerful. Plants are a perfect embodiment of the four elements: earth, air, water, and fire. Plants are earth, but also utilize sun (fire), water, and air to thrive. In addition to embodying the four elements, every plant comes with its own set of magickal correspondences and uses. See the reference guide on the opposite page for more information about common plants used in ritual and the magickal properties they possess.

LAVENDER
Peace + Awareness

CINNAMON
Energy + Manifesting

CEDAR
Grounding + Strength

MUGWORT
Magick + Intuition

ROSEMARY
Health + Clearing

CLOVE
Protection + Authority

ROSE
Beauty + Love

BASIL
Prosperity + Confidence

GARDEN SAGE
Purification + Healing

YARROW
Attraction + Dreamwork

BAY LEAF
Focus + Success

MINT
Clarity + Inspiration

BURNING HERBS

One of the most common uses for herbs in cultures all over the world is burning them for smoke cleansing. The ceremonial burning of herbs is an ancient tradition that continues to be practiced by a wide variety of cultures and religions today. You don't need anything fancy to perform your own herb-burning ritual. Herbs can be burned loose in a fireproof vessel like a cauldron or an abalone shell, or they can be wrapped into stick form and burned. Here are some of the benefits of burning herbs:

1. Cleanse negative energy.

2. Protect your space.

3. Cleanse your aura.

4. Bring positive energy.

5. Balance the elements within your space.

6. Cleanse the air (many herbs have an antimicrobial effect).

7. Consecrate items.

8. Simply for the aroma!

Side note: A word on cultural appropriation. The use of the word *smudge* by non-Indigenous Americans to describe general herb burning is both inaccurate and hurtful. Here are some simple alternatives: smoke cleansing, herb burning, and herb stick. In this same vein, I encourage anyone using herbs for magickal purposes to do so responsibly. Consider using plants for cleansing from your own cultural heritage. Though white sage is very popular for burning, it is also overharvested. There are a variety of herbs that can be just as powerful, more environmentally friendly, and not harmful to Indigenous communities. Any of the herbs listed on page 111 can be used as a replacement for white sage.

·◁〜 **WORKING WITH PLANTS IN RITUAL** 〜▷·

There are a variety of ways to use plants and herbs in your ritual practice. Plants and herbs can be used in charm bags, spell bottles, teas, and herbal baths. In fact, simply having them present can be beneficial. Unlike when burning herbs, herbs used for spellwork can be fresh, dried, or in essential oil form depending on how you plan to use them. Start experimenting with adding herbs to your magickal practice.

·◦ゝ TIP ゟ◦·

Herbs are medicine and should be used with care and caution. Be sure to check with a medical professional before ingesting, inhaling, using on skin, or creating a tea bath using any herbs you're unfamiliar with.

What goals or projects are you trying to accomplish at this moment? Imagine how you would feel once they are completed and write about it here.

*What herbs do you feel will help get you closer to
your current goals? How so?*

PROTECTION CHARM BAGS

Charm bags are a simple way to create a portable magick spell. Follow these steps to complete your protection charm bag.

You'll need:

- Mugwort
- Clove
- Salt
- Amethyst
- Marker
- Cloth bag

Instructions:

1. Collect the herbs and crystals listed above, just enough to put in your bag—a teaspoon or so will do, but you don't need to be exact. It's okay if you don't have all of the ingredients; use what you have.

2. Cleanse all of your items with cleansing smoke, then hold each one in your hand and ask for it to help offer you energetic protection.

3. Draw or paint an Algiz Rune on the front of your bag. (See page 102 for an example of this Rune.)

4. Hold the bag in your hands and repeat, "I call on the energy of these sacred items, my guides, and well ancestors to protect me from anything not meant for me." You may also decide to end with something like "so it is" or "so mote it be" if it feels good to do so.

5. Place your charm bag anywhere you'd like to feel better protected.

*What is a current fear that's keeping you from taking a
step toward your desires?*

How would it feel to not carry this fear? How would it change your actions to not carry this fear?

What goals or projects are you trying to accomplish at this moment?
Imagine how you will feel once they are completed and write about it here.

⬧ CANDLE MAGICK ⬧

If you are interested in beginning to practice spellwork but aren't quite sure where to begin, candle magick is the perfect jumping-off point. Candle magick is a great tool for manifesting because it's all about setting intentions and visualizing outcomes. Candles also represent all four elements, making them a potent source of intention setting. The solid wax and the wick of the candle symbolize earth, the flame represents fire, the smoke represents air, and the melting wax represents water.

Candle magick rituals require you to focus on specific goals and visualize both their implementation and their outcome. Intense visualization often stirs up a variety of emotions, which will help you connect more deeply with your desires. Think of the candle as a communicator between yourself and the Universe. As the candle burns, it beams your goals and intentions out into the world.

You can perform candle magick with just about any candle, but you may find that you prefer specific types of candles for specific spells. I prefer to use paraffin wax spell candles (sometimes called chime candles) because they are made specifically for candle magick, are affordable, are readily available, and have a short burn time of 45 to 60 minutes.

Any candle will do. The color of your candle also has an impact on your ritual or spell. Check out the candle color guide on the opposite page to learn how each color can influence your intention.

⊰⌣ CANDLE COLORS ⌣⊱

BLACK
Protection

PINK
Love

BLUE
Peace

ORANGE
Creativity

BROWN
Balance

GREEN
Abundance

YELLOW
Confidence

SILVER
Intuition

GOLD
Good Fortune

WHITE
New Beginnings

VIOLET
Spirituality

RED
Passion

HOW TO PREPARE YOUR CANDLES

Before you begin, you'll want to cleanse and anoint your candle. Here's how to cleanse your candle.

1. Inspect your candle for any physical signs of dirt or dust and ensure that your candle is physically clean.

2. Cleanse the energy of your candle with herbal smoke (see page 112) or by wiping it down with water.

3. *Optional:* Anoint your candle with an oil of choice. This step gives you the opportunity to imprint your energy onto the candle after it's been cleansed. Simple oils like almond, olive, or coconut work great. Put a couple drops of oil on your hands and rub it on the candle. If using essential oil, always ensure it's diluted and safe for skin contact.

4. As you rub the candle with oil, focus on your desired outcome and imagine your energy being absorbed by the candle.

5. Don't have any oil handy? Simply hold the candle in your hands as you imprint it with your energy.

Do this candle ritual to help you manifest your desires.

1. Select a candle color that is in alignment with your intention. It's always best to perform candle magick with a new candle.

2. Cleanse and anoint your candle, while visualizing your intention.

3. *Optional:* Before lighting your candle, roll it in herbs that correspond with your desired outcome and place corresponding crystals around your candle (revisit herb correspondences on page 111 and crystals on page 149).

4. Light your candle while focusing on your intention. Always use good sense while working with fire. Never leave your candle or a flame unattended.

5. The candle-burning process could mean gazing at your candle, meditating, dancing and moving, or performing a card reading as it burns. Whatever you decide to do, ensure that your intention is top of mind. It is ideal to allow the candle to burn fully in one sitting. If you decide to space out the candle burning over several nights, don't blow out your candle. Instead, snuff it out with a candle snuffer. The candle snuffer will help seal your intent rather than blowing it away.

6. Be mindful over the coming day(s) of how this exercise makes you feel about the intention you've set for yourself.

What was your intention for your first candle spell?
What color did you select and why?

In what ways do you feel differently about your intention
after completing this candle spell?

What insights have you gained about the intention you set since performing your candle spell?

_____

_____

_____

_____

_____

_____

_____

_____

_____

_____

_____

_____

_____

···◆ MAGICKAL DAYS ◆···

Did you know that the days of the week can affect the energy of your rituals? Each day of the week has its own energy that can be harnessed to enhance your rituals and spellwork. Understanding each day's particular energetic properties can help you boost the effectiveness of your magick. Don't worry too much if your rituals and your days aren't always in sync. Performing a ritual on a particular day will not make or break it, but it can help push your intentions in the direction you desire most.

Each day of the week carries either an outward energy (often called masculine) or an inward energy (often called feminine), as well as the energy of a planet and an element. Here's a little more detail about each day and how you can use it to your advantage.

⊸⌣ DAYS OF THE WEEK ⌣⊳

·●☽ SUNDAY ☾●·

(Outward/Masculine)
Growth, personal power, goals
Planet: Sun (ego and motivation)
Element: Fire (passion and courage)

·●☽ MONDAY ☾●·

(Inward/Feminine)
Intuitive work, increased psychic abilities, emotion
Planet: Moon (emotions and intuition)
Element: Water (peace and healing)

·•☾ TUESDAY ☽•·

(Outward/Masculine)
Strength, courage, leadership
Planet: Mars (action and strength)
Element: Fire (passion and courage)

·•☾ WEDNESDAY ☽•·

(Outward/Masculine)
Creativity, change, communication
Planet: Mercury (intellect and communication)
Element: Air (joy and imagination)

·•☾ THURSDAY ☽•·

(Outward/Masculine)
Abundance, wealth, success
Planet: Jupiter (philosophy and expansion)
Element: Earth (grounded and logical)

·•☾ FRIDAY ☽•·

(Inward/Feminine)
Love, romance, fertility
Planet: Venus (love and relationships)
Element: Water (peace and healing)

·•☾ SATURDAY ☽•·

(Inward/Feminine)
Protection, cleansing, endings
Planet: Saturn (ambition and boundaries)
Element: Earth (grounded and logical),
Fire (passion and courage)

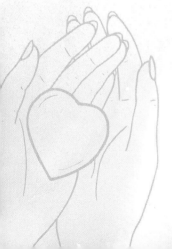

·•◗ SUNDAY ◖•·

Spend some time thinking about your week ahead. Write a plan for each day that you feel excited about.

Make time to tune into your intuition with a tool of choice. Write down your experience here. How did it feel to build in time for intuitive work on a Monday?

·•◊ TUESDAY ◊•·

Write down a project you want to start and the first three things you need to do to get going on it. Try to complete your list. How did it feel to begin working toward this goal?

Write out a conversation you've been meaning to have with someone.

·⦿◗ THURSDAY ◖⦿·

Reflect on everything that's transpired this week. Write down an expression of gratitude in your journal.

·∘◊ FRIDAY ◊∘·

How does your heart feel today? Make a list of ways you can cultivate more love and pleasure.

·◦◊ SATURDAY ◁◦·

Energetically cleanse yourself and your space using a method of choice. How do you and your space feel after you've made time to cleanse the energy?

···•◇ MOON PHASES ◇•···

The phases of the Moon are synonymous with the Triple Goddess—or the Maiden, Mother, and Crone. The Maiden is represented by the Waxing Moon, and she embodies purity, youth, creation, pleasure, naivety, and new beginnings. The Mother is represented by the Full Moon, and she embodies love, fertility, nourishment, responsibility, patience, and self-care. The Crone is represented by the Waning Moon, and she embodies fulfillment, endings, wisdom, death, and rebirth.

If Mother Moon pulls the tides, imagine how strong her influence is on your mind and body! She can affect your mood, physical body, and spirit body. Journaling alongside the phases of the Moon can help you uncover patterns in your day-to-day life. You may find that you're more in sync with the Moon than you thought. You may find that your diet, intuition, and menstruation are affected by the phases of the Moon. The best way to know how the Moon affects you is to journal regularly.

There are simple and powerful rituals you can do for each Moon phase to harness and honor its power. Follow the phases of the Moon for practicing specific rituals. Do abundance and manifesting work as the Moon grows from waxing to full. Practice letting go and releasing as the Moon wanes.

MOON PHASE MEANINGS

NEW
MOON
Cleanse

WAXING
CRESCENT
Declare

FIRST
QUARTER
Act

WAXING
GIBBOUS
Refine

FULL
MOON
Celebrate

WANING
GIBBOUS
Accept

LAST
QUARTER
Release

WANING
CRESCENT
Reflect

DARK
MOON
Integrate

◄◡ FULL MOONS BY MONTHS ◡►

The Full Moon is a special time, but this was especially true for ancient people, because the phases of the Moon helped delineate the passage of time and seasons. A Full Moon, usually, happens just once a month, so it was an important marker in the cycle.

Over the span of human history, different cultures have associated a variety of names and meanings with the Full Moon of each month. The names given to each Full Moon can vary quite a bit from culture to culture, which is why names differ from source to source.

The names for each Full Moon remain the same year after year, barring a couple of exceptions. A second Full Moon in any month is called a Blue Moon.

JANUARY—WOLF MOON
Renewal

FEBRUARY—ICE MOON
Strength

MARCH—WORM MOON
Emergence

APRIL—PINK MOON
Fertility

MAY—FLOWER MOON
Growth

JUNE—STRAWBERRY MOON
Bending

JULY—WORT MOON
Gathering

AUGUST—CORN MOON
Peace

SEPTEMBER—HARVEST MOON
Celebration

OCTOBER—BLOOD MOON
Protection

NOVEMBER—SNOW MOON
Observance

DECEMBER—OAK MOON
Hope

What would you like to bring more of into your life? Which Moon phase do you think would help you align best with your desires?

How could you honor the upcoming Full Moon based on its theme? How could you apply the upcoming Full Moon's theme to your life?

Which Moon phase and archetype (Waxing/Maiden, Full/Mother, Waning/Crone) do you feel you have the most to learn from, and why?

·•☽ TRACK YOUR MOOD ☾•·

Keep track of your mood during each phase here. You can search the Moon phases with an app, a calendar, or online.

Moon Phase: _____   Moon Phase: _____

Date: _____   Date: _____

Mood: _____   Mood: _____

Moon Phase: _____   Moon Phase: _____

Date: _____   Date: _____

Mood: _____   Mood: _____

Moon Phase: _____   Moon Phase: _____

Date: _____   Date: _____

Mood: _____   Mood: _____

Moon Phase: _____   Moon Phase: _____

Date: _____   Date: _____

Mood: _____   Mood: _____

Moon Phase: _____   Moon Phase: _____

Date: _____   Date: _____

Mood: _____   Mood: _____

Moon Phase: _____   Moon Phase: _____

Date: _____   Date: _____

Mood: _____   Mood: _____

Moon Phase: _____   Moon Phase: _____

Date: _____   Date: _____

Mood: _____   Mood: _____

Moon Phase: _____   Moon Phase: _____

Date: _____   Date: _____

Mood: _____   Mood: _____

Moon Phase: _____   Moon Phase: _____

Date: _____   Date: _____

Mood: _____   Mood: _____

Moon Phase: _____   Moon Phase: _____

Date: _____   Date: _____

Mood: _____   Mood: _____

Moon Phase: _____   Moon Phase: _____

Date: _____   Date: _____

Mood: _____   Mood: _____

After tracking your mood during each Moon phase, in which Moon phase did you notice that you felt the best? In which Moon phase did you feel the worst or with low energy?

How could you modify your schedule or build in more self-care to feel better during Moon phases that are more challenging for you?

···◇ CRYSTALS ◇···

Crystals are energetic powerhouses that can absorb negative energy, calm you, and be programmed with your desires. Similar to herbs, days of the week, and the phases of the Moon, each crystal carries a unique energy. One of the most alluring qualities of crystals is that they're wearable and easily transportable. Think of them as an energetic intention in your pocket!

Crystals are comprised of perfectly repeated atoms. The flawless arrangement of energy within crystals is their superpower. They radiate this energy outward, and anything within their range can benefit. Their unique arrangement also makes them ideal for storing information and energy, which is what makes them such a powerful intention-setting tool.

When using crystals as an intention-setting tool, you're relying on the power of your mind to initiate change; the crystal serves as a reminder of the change you want to create. The healing properties associated with each crystal can serve as a reminder to act in a way that's in alignment with your desires. Be curious about which crystals attract your attention the most. Ask yourself which ones feel right to you.

YOU MAY FIND THAT WHAT YOU'RE DRAWN TO IS WHAT YOU NEED THE MOST.

You can work with crystals in several different ways, and the following is a quick summary.

- ◆ **Keep your crystals nearby.** Place them on your body, your nightstand while you sleep, your desk while you work, or wear them.

- ◆ **Program your crystal with desired energy.** While holding your crystal, imagine your desires going into the crystal. Your programmed crystal will serve as a potent reminder of goals and intentions.

- ◆ **Create crystal grids.** Placing multiple crystals in a circular and balanced pattern can amplify their power and your intentions. Select one center stone and five to ten secondary stones that correspond with your intention. Visualize your intention while placing each stone in a circular pattern.

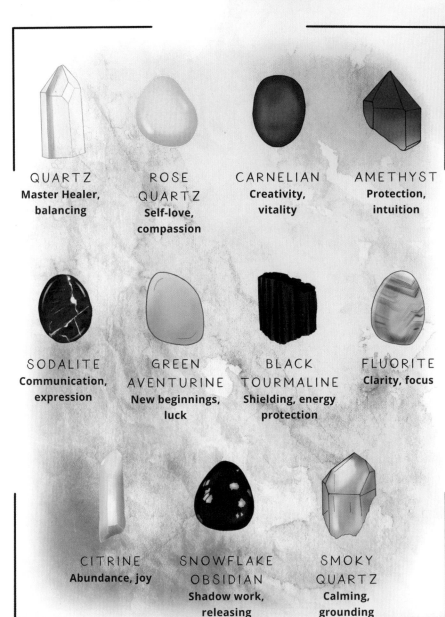

QUARTZ
Master Healer,
balancing

ROSE QUARTZ
Self-love,
compassion

CARNELIAN
Creativity,
vitality

AMETHYST
Protection,
intuition

SODALITE
Communication,
expression

GREEN AVENTURINE
New beginnings,
luck

BLACK TOURMALINE
Shielding, energy
protection

FLUORITE
Clarity, focus

CITRINE
Abundance, joy

SNOWFLAKE OBSIDIAN
Shadow work,
releasing

SMOKY QUARTZ
Calming,
grounding

HOW TO CLEANSE YOUR CRYSTALS

Your crystals will pick up energy from you, your space, and other people, so it's important to cleanse them regularly. Here are a few simple ways to do this:

♦ Run them under water.

♦ Go over them with a cleansing herb of choice.

♦ Place them in sunlight for five to ten minutes (some stones, like amethyst and fluorite, can fade in sunlight, so don't keep them outside for too long).

♦ Imagine the crystals being cleared on an energetic level as you cleanse them. Do this as often as you feel called to. If you're unsure when to do this, monthly is always a good idea.

PROTECTION CRYSTAL GRID RITUAL

Use this crystal grid to offer yourself and your space energetic protection.

- ♦ **Sacred geometry:** Metratron's cube.

- ♦ **Affirmation:** My energy is safe and protected.

- ♦ **Center stone:** Raw or tumbled black tourmaline.

- ♦ **Secondary stones:** Hematite, amethyst, labradorite.

Instructions:

1. Cleanse your crystals (see page 150).

2. Place your largest gemstone in the center and arrange your other stones radiating out evenly around it.

3. As you place each stone, repeat the affirmation and visualize a shield of light enveloping you and the space.

4. Using your finger, trace over the top of each stone while visualizing the energy connecting and radiating outward.

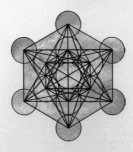

After completing the crystal grid ritual on page 151, spend five to ten minutes connecting with your breath and body and notice the energy of this grid. How do you feel now that the grid is complete? Do you notice any shifts or changes in your energy?

Amethyst is great to guide your intuition. Hold an amethyst in your hand, then ask the crystal to guide you on your next step. What is something that you have been struggling with and what is your intuition telling you about how to move forward?

Citrine is a great crystal to have around to draw more abundance to your life. While holding a piece of citrine, think about areas of your life in which you'd like to feel more abundant. Ask for guidance from your citrine stone for affirmations and write them out here.

Affirmation:

Affirmation:

Affirmation:

Carry or have a sodalite nearby to inspire clear communication and self-expression. Write a letter to yourself about a time in which you were truly happy, as if you were telling a story to someone for the first time.

NEW BEGINNINGS RITUAL

Green aventurine is a stone of new beginnings and luck. It corresponds with the New Moon and is an ideal stone for beginning a new path or journey.

You'll need:

- ♦ Timing: New Moon
- ♦ Green aventurine
- ♦ Paper
- ♦ Pen or pencil
- ♦ *Optional:* white candle

Instructions:

1. Write down the new path or journey you'd like to begin on your piece of paper. If you're using a white candle, you can light it now.

2. Hold your paper and your green aventurine in your hands and visualize embarking on this new path. Notice how you feel and think about how you'd like it to go.

3. Place your paper under your green aventurine and keep it there until the Full Moon. Try to make contact with it daily.

4. After the Full Moon you can bury or recycle the paper, trusting that your path will unfold in your highest good.

What new path or journey do you intend to take? How did it feel to visualize it unfolding?

What will you do today or in the next few days to begin your new path or journey?

···◆ ABOUT THE AUTHOR ◆···

Cassie Uhl is an intuitive energy healer, founder of her former business Zenned Out, and the author of seven books and two card decks. She combines her love of spirituality, creativity, and teaching to offer readers beautiful and accessible information about various spiritual topics through her books, blog, and podcast, *Awen*. She is passionate about helping others feel supported as they begin or deepen their spiritual journey.

Cassie opened up to her spiritual gifts at a young age through meditation and working with her energy. She had a supportive, open-minded grandmother who made her feel safe to explore her spirituality. This foundation helped her become a compassionate guide to those who feel stuck, unsure, or even anxious about the next step in their spiritual journeys. Her healing practice offers a trauma-informed approach to energy healing, journeying, intuitive mentorship, and end-of-life doula services.

Cassie is the author of the Zenned Out Series of books: *The Zenned Out Guide to Understanding Auras*, *The Zenned Out Guide to Understanding Chakras*, *The Zenned Out Guide to Understanding Crystals*, *The Zenned Out Guide to Understanding the Wheel of the Year*, *The Zenned Out Guide to Understanding Tarot*, and the tarot kit, *The Zenned Out Journey Tarot*. Learn more about Cassie and her offerings at **cassieuhl.com**.

Inspiring | Educating | Creating | Entertaining

Brimming with creative inspiration, how-to projects, and useful information to enrich your everyday life, quarto.com is a favorite destination for those pursuing their interests and passions.

© 2023 by Quarto Publishing Group USA Inc.
Text and Illustrations © 2023 by Cassandra Uhl

First published in 2023 by Rock Point,
an imprint of The Quarto Group,
142 West 36th Street, 4th Floor
New York, NY 10018, USA
T (212) 779-4972 F (212) 779-6058
www.Quarto.com

Rock Point titles are also available at discount for retail, wholesale, promotional, and bulk purchase. For details, contact the Special Sales Manager by email at specialsales@quarto.com or by mail at The Quarto Group, Attn: Special Sales Manager, 100 Cummings Center Suite 265D, Beverly, MA 01915 USA.

10 9 8 7 6 5 4 3 2 1

ISBN: 978-1-63106-900-0

PUBLISHER: Rage Kindelsperger
CREATIVE DIRECTOR: Laura Drew
MANAGING EDITOR: Cara Donaldson
EDITOR: Keyla Pizarro-Hernández
COVER AND INTERIOR DESIGN: Sydney Martenis

Printed in China